DANCING ON EDGE
THE McREDEYE POEMS

ART GOODTIMES

LITHIC PRESS
FRUITA, COLORADO

DANCING ON EDGE
Copyright © 2019 Art Goodtimes
All rights reserved.

Cover art by Wendy Videlock
Layout by Kyle Harvey

DANCING ON EDGE
ART GOODTIMES
ISBN 978-1946-583-147
Lithic Press

LITHIC PRESS
fine books for an old planet

www.lithicpress.com

Dedicated to Jack's Gang: Wendy Videlock, Danny Rosen, Kyle Harvey, Rosemerry Wahtola Trommer & the Budada hisself

CONTENTS

ars BIOGRAFICA   15

Patriarchy   17
Catholic San Francisco   18
Learned Errors & Unbidden Catechisms   19
Smoking   20
Ethically Ill-Suited   21
Incompatability   23
Divorces   24
Doing the Paleohip   25
Still   26
Sileo   27
Dying   28

ars RELAZIONI   31

Make Peace   33
Picking Red   34
The Day I Heard the News   35
Dove Creek   36
Budada Buddies   38

ars POLITICA   41

Colorado   43
Our Dark Milky Way   44
Seven Billion & Growing   46
San Miguel Resource Center   47
Embers   48
Exceptional   49
On Laying Around Unattached   50
De Natura   51
Contra Bookchin   52
To Hell You Ride   55
Downhill Slide   56

Winter of Our Discontent 58
Happy Everything 60

ars POETICA 63

Fountain Pen 65
On One's Own 66
Ikkyū in Berg's *Crow With No Mouth* 67
Yin Yang 68
A Diction Airy 69

ars PHILOSOPHIAE 71

Boxtop Wisdom Aside 73
Honey I Got That Ice Age Hunger 74
The Edge 76
Being 77
Drought 78
Paganus 79
Blood Moon 80
Moral Compass Amble 81
Officiating 82
Who Who Who 83

ars ALLEATIeSIMBIONTI 85

Kindom Canticle 87
Tree Metaphysics 89
Tipping the World 91
Deer 93
Cannabaloney 94
No Don't Do the New 95
Entheogens Take You Away 97

ars TOPOGRAFIE   99

Lost Coast   101
California   103
Colorado Coyote   105
Sunset Ridge   106
Whiteout in the Canyon   108
Mt. Blanca   110
Gusty Winds   111
Sorcerer's Apprentice   112
Memento Mori   113
13,019   114
Shivaree   115

DANCING ON EDGE
THE McREDEYE POEMS

> *"Every so often you have to wake up &*
> *jump off a cliff."* –Utah Phillips

I was born on the edges … At the final cliffs of all our species' wanderings, as Lew Welch sang … Born in the Mission District, not far from the sorrows of Mission Dolores where the Franciscans herded the *indígena* of Yerba Buena into servitude, disease and near annihilation … Born on the far leftish bank of the Haight-Ashbury's San Andreas Fault, as it rips its slow-mo way north from Mexico through bear flag California and cyber-sophisticate Silicon Valley … Born to a mixed breed *familia* of immigrant Italians, proper Anglicans, Gaelic outcasts and dispossessed Spaniards.

According to ethnographers, a fragment of a song of the ancestors of the present day Muwekma Ohlone Tribe survived the Indigenous genocide -- "Dancing on the brink of the world" … Those ancient ones lived life during the Bay Area's post-glacial Holocene -- one of the most densely populated native regions of pre-conquest Turtle Island … Dancing. Singing. Hunting. Fishing … Thriving for thousands of years.

It took me a while to learn to dance … Religion claimed me early – first-born son of an immigrant bombardier Knight of Columbus … Mama wrote in my baby book that I'd make a great priest … But I didn't … I left the seminary … Left the Church … Found the redneck West as a government do-gooder on a reservation in Montana … And came back home post-VISTA to San Francisco's Summer of Love as a Conscientious Objector to the Vietnam disaster.

Tossed, taken and transformulated in the entheogenic trance of the Sixties, I began to dance … And to sing … I found my voice as a poet, attempting to speak the beauty and horror of place -- as history's valley oaks dropped leaves from the tree of knowledge and curled them at my feet … As relict groves of redwood goddesses ascended into the mist of the Santa Cruz Mountains and strummed their unearthly lyres.

Moving to Colorado to start a family, I found myself on another edge … Found myself on the shores of an ancient inland sea that had turned to sandstone, a slickrock landscape punctuated by volcanic extrusions … Found myself in a nation edging into world dominance and weighed down with the Cold War burden of empire … Found myself at a time when nuclear cataclysm seemed more karmic inevitability than mere sci-fi nightmare … I was seven years old before television came into my life, and the first image I can recall, vibrating through the vacuum tubes of our black & white Philco, was our country's mushroom cloud bomb-burst test over Bikini atoll.

Radicalized in joining the all-star eco-backfield of Earth First!, I met Dolores LaChapelle and was gifted with the opportunity to understand reciprocal appropriation and sacred land/sacred sex from her Way of the Mountain sanctuary in the San Juan Mountains … To dance with opposites … To take. To give back. To worship at the altars of an animate universe … In Telluride I became a local elected Green official, and had to shape my Rainbow Family ideals and Deep Ecology philosophy to the flawed and imperfect reality of American democracy, with its hopeful rhetoric, if inconsistently progressive practice.

In the process, I found myself in dialogue with McRedeye, a guardian consort, an alter echo, a character of my leaping imagination, analogous to Lew Welch's Red Monk … These poems are an evolving record of the horizontal gene transfer in those conversations.

ars BIOGRAFICA

"All power to the paradox."

–Jack Mueller, *Amor Fati*
(Lithic Press, 2013)

PATRIARCHY

Vincenzo was a mama's boy
From him I learned
the feminine

How to be charming
Go into the business of
being liked. He fucked every gal

in sight, or on the side & then
like grandpa did *la familia*
he abandoned them

Blanche hung
her father's bootstraps
like hickeys round her neck

Shamed me & the bros
Had Dad whip us
with a belt when bad

Taught me early on
to love books
Just what her drunken

pater familias had beat her
for bringing home
from school

McRedeye sez
It's not so much
her scars

As the scare of
men
that stung

CATHOLIC SAN FRANCISCO

Born at St. Luke's
Holy patron of artists
doctors & butchers

On Army Street in the Mission
which got converted
to César Chávez Street

Then baptized at
St. Paul of the Shipwreck
Capsized

before he'd even launched
amid Bayview's
truck farmers & albino outcasts

Memorized rote Latin
& corny joke Greek
at St. Joe's seminary

Almost tonsured
at St. Pat's but
before that, deselected

Not the most auspicious
of starts
McRedeye sez

Ending the Sixties
a twisted little quakie
bouncing round the Haight

But, godsakes, potted
plumped & ready
to rock 'n' roll

LEARNED ERRORS &
UNBIDDEN CATECHISMS

I came to orgasm
in a dream, McRedeye sez

As a squirt I sensed sex
in the curl of cigarette
smoke

Woke up wet at 13
Imagining a locomotive
steaming down the track

And an ur-Aphrodite's lips
voluptuously swallowing
the smokestack

But Christian quick
Mama hissed. "Don't touch!"

Me caught
squirming in the pews
Trying to rejigger a stiffie
in my tight Sunday slacks

So's anytime, anywhere
playing with myself

I learned to be
appropriately ashamed

As if denial were virtue
& only sin delight

SMOKING

Smoking gal
Smoking car
McRedeye sez

Hard
can turn you on
as much as soft

ETHICALLY ILL-SUITED

Orange buckets
like hurricane scatter
clog the clutter

Worksites in progress
Odd yard jobs abandoned
Clumped exotic castoffs
half-assembled

Staircases of nudes
descending like mirrors with
broken chocolate grinders
under their arms

Trying to live a life of
voluntary do-plicity
he says

Simple but sure-footed
amid the tar pits of the century
Making do with whatever's
available overflow

Reinhabiting
a house with a history

on one townsite acre
split off from the McKee Ranch
near the corner of Colo. Hwy. 145
& Lone Cone Road

Planting trees
Harvesting apples & potatoes

"Looks like Little Appalachia"
McRedeye sneers
"A hippie Rainbow's voluntary publicity"

Electricity but no running water
on a straw-bale acre where they reuse
Repurpose. Warehouse whatever's been
picked up & might become valuable

Obedient to the Mountains
Mindful of cycles of surplus & want
fill & flush, drought & flood

Boxes. Papers. Books. Odd hats
collected as curator to pass on singularities
to those who come next

"You're a hoarder," my son says
"Not an archivist"

And maybe it's true
That's a jumpsuit I'm wearing
The sky tattoo'd day-glo on my sleeves

Swimming solo
in a coral pool of stinging
jello

INCOMPATIBILITY

My pickup's got a fever
sez McRedeye. I'm

overheated & she's lipstick
in the front seat, yelling

lawyers, lugnuts, alimony
All the way to the bank

DIVORCES

I know now I'm not exempt
But I didn't know enough then
not to make the obvious mistakes
Marrying for all the old reasons

The first, for getting her pregnant

The second, for letting her tears
divert me from the solo odyssey
I never got to embark on

The third, for refusing
to hear or see evil
in spite of the early warning signs

Like her falling down
drunk in the barrow ditch

Or, was I bewitched?

The fourth
(although we only separated)
for mistaking
kindness for love
compassion for passion

And so
I've finally come
to learn, McRedeye sez

not to embrace
the wounded feminine

& foolishly expect
the thousand-armed Goddess
not to retaliate

DOING THE PALEOHIP

"I'm not so sure
the sacred I was taught
ain't pure bullshit"
McRedeye sez

Though the Maya remind
"Thank Ixchel for hallucinogens"

'Cept still not clear
who's on top
tier this mind round

The old fears
toss wrenches in the way
as the dynamos start
their slow decay

Young, we swung freely
from epiphany to party

But aging can be
a dangerously vicious habit
of becoming increasingly
decrepit

Seniors at the center
wolfing down a free lunch
before pills & appointments

How about, instead
accepting the flicker feather
mantle & tale hoop of an elder

Bagging the snipe
the kids can't find

STILL

Rainbow old age's
a paradoxically newsome place
a curious toe finds itself in

Seems the bellbottom
semelparity of the Sixties
hides its retro radioactive flair
in see-through pools

In an uptight overheated
millennium of
uncool

But I can't stop
tasting the waters
Testing for shark

Yes I will swallow fire
Kiss karma's ruby lips

Still
McRedeye sez
I miss hip's chill

SILEO

On 11 Aug 2008 at 15:55,
Hot Carr wrote:
Silence,
it's noisy in here

McRedeye sez

Yep, it's there at the center
Just after annoyance
& those jazz riff
peripherals

Nada completo's
whole enchilada

Enchanted in *silencio*

Sileo, silere -- to be
quiet. Be still
Gently at rest with

Or maybe
it's being at peace with
what's left unsaid

Watching as I dıd
Dad's last breath

DYING

"You see, we are all sentenced to die"
-Steve Clark

The cancer's in us too
of course. But when it
climbs out of its skin cage

& starts attacking
Torturing
Blowing things up

Beheading the body
What can we do
but fight

Joke. Curse. Cry
& then let the malignancy
have its way

as it will
running its course
Fine, McRedeye sez

When it's time, let's
kiss it goodbye. This world
All those we've kissed

ars RELAZIONI

"Li, then, is rather the order and pattern in Nature, not formulated Law. But it is not pattern thought of as something dead, like a mosaic; it is a dynamic pattern as embodied in all living things, and in human relationships and in the highest human values."

-Joseph Needham, *The Grand Titration*
(Allen & Unwin, 1969)

MAKE PEACE

Is it maturity
to have moved from
outlaw to in-law?

To've shed
the stars & stripes scarf
of Earth First's motto
"No Compromise"

For a political pacemaker
For a seat on the board
as peacemaker

Shoulder-to-shoulder
with enemies & allies
milling around & working
the Radical Middle

Or is it simply
a failure of nerve?

This unwillingness
to allow the Other
in all her guises
all his gyrations

not to become
our friends

Or perhaps, McRedeye sez
it's that grand
hardscrabble mistake of
learning love last

PICKING RED

—for Kit Kalriess Muldoon

There it was. A red kerchief left
in the Denver Museum parking
lot. Unclaimed. Run over

Do I stoop to pick it up
& wave its dust aloft
into my floating world?

A gesture, maybe. Like Kit's
All in red, sharing the Merc's
center stage with the Erotic

Or conjuring stone soup
for sodden poets in the San
Juan shelter of her worn van

Making more than just
do, with meager pickings
Making a feast. That's it!

That's Kit, McRedeye sez
Making a feast of adversities
And for us, in our sadnesses

it's picking up on the red
brilliance she's left us
Not dead cloth left behind

THE DAY I HEARD THE NEWS

—for Stan Abrams

They were rolling up the last bales
from the hayfields' first cutting
A wet spring's guarantee of more

to come. Like the water
that will always come out of
the upper basin micro-storage

pond he'd built on Turkey Creek
Like the sun always seeking closure
& tonight beams of golden tabernacle

flame erupting from the La Sals
against the polygamous underbellies
of the low-slung rainclouds

high-flyin' pink flamingo cirrus
& the cascading cumuli of a backlit
thunderhead. It's like the western

sky's playing him pipe organ
Picking the Toccata from Widor's
Fifth as the Sun's recessional

Slipping away unseen but on cue
McRedeye sez. His 8-ball
scratched in death's pocket

DOVE CREEK

"Hey friend," Ernie grins
He wants a favor

We've been pols in adjoining counties
ten years or so now
Different parties. Redneck & hippie
But we've often found a way
to help each other out

"Write me a poem"
he says
"about odd friends"

And McRedeye
howls with laughter

We've all come to know
you don't always get to dance
with the one you came with

"Odd friends?"
I chime in
"Ain't that the truth, Ernie"

And there's no denying
some of the most virulent
opinionated
hardcore issue opponents
I've tussled with & lost to
in some public fora
or other

& even a few half-soused
jock-talk bigmouths I've met
in conference hospitality suites
have turned out to be
quite charming souls

Not opposed to
goodness

Maybe a little twisted

Wind-whipped
like a grain elevator
gone to seed

Or yellow tractors
chained to their rusts

So, why is it
McRedeye wonders
some of the odd people you
fast forward friend in life
can be crazy bi-polar
opposites
you never would have
expected to nod to
on the street

Let alone
trust like a sister
Like a brother

BUDADA BUDDIES

So, McRedeye sez
I magnetized her missive
to my new refrigerator door

Slapping on a top-heavy
bottle-opener stick'em
to grip the paper

Its metal body kilt
all decked out in strawberry
kitsch & cream

I watched as
the envelope's inscription
in her Brazilian scrawl
started
inching downwards

Turning my name
like my life
upside down

ars POLITICA

"Traveler, this is no fountain.
Wounded, I am no healer.
Hungry, not one word here
is as good as bread."

-Naomi Replansky,
Collected Poems (Black Sparrow, 2012)

COLORADO

Hey, McRedeye sez
I'm no pacifist saint

I eat meat, swat
mosquitos, usually on sight

Even as a Conscientious Objector
I personally couldn't stand by
& watch thugs of any stripe
take down women & children

There is a life worse than death

But count me out of
pre-emptive strikes, drone attacks
all those boosters of foreign wars

I didn't have to
ship out to 'Nam to know hell
I've heard the stories
Imagined the nightmares

In self-defense
or to protect the weak
I'd kill

But not until they invade
Colorado

OUR DARK MILKY WAY

Knew I'd blown all claim to
sustainability's bully pulpit
when I said yes
to a third biological

Not to mention my three
step-sired little darlings

But McRedeye sez
when it comes to off-spring
& embedded
who would choose
to wriggle away from love?

The world really matters!

Not just its gaseous secrets
Its bosons, charms & anti-quarks
But the whole minestrone

Even our hot flash blips
on one brief planet's
backwater spark
within galaxies spiraling
darkly into oblivion

We know our Milky Way's
countless stars of superheated
plasma will one day go
supernova

Disappear in a multiverse of dwarf
blues & giant yellows
Easter eggs
in the void's black basket

Each mysterious sparkle of life
weaves a wormhole flicker
into gravity's taut warp

SEVEN BILLION & GROWING

Dolores LaChapelle always said
it was like we were living through
a bomb blast in slow motion

Turns one invertebrate, so
you can hardly feel the water
boil. The veins burst

In just
one generation's rinky-dink spin
going from Three Billion to
Seven Billion & growing
exponentially

A virus
A crash population. A species
koyaanistkatsi

Whom, asks McRedeye
do you think could
get us back in synch?

A Hitler? A Stalin?
A Pope? A President?
A woman in her garden?

SAN MIGUEL
RESOURCE CENTER

970-728-5660

Black eye. Hickies
Eggplant bruises
on arms & thighs

McRedeye sez
Some hammer a dent
into a hoop

& call it heart
If that's your Valentine
call the hotline

EMBERS

Christmas lights here
Christmas lights there
Pretty soon

the yurt wears a rainbow
strand of twinkling pearls
day & night

The studio sports
a peace symbol the size of
a gas station logo

Lit up chili peppers
heat the kitchen. Angel
Illuminati haunt the porch

But for the life of me
McRedeye sez
all I can see are

embers
of a thousand chunks of coal
exploding into ash

EXCEPTIONAL

What keeps
America
exceptional?

Its looks?
Its legs?
Or its arms?

McRedeye sez
Don't ask

ON LAYING AROUND UNATTACHED

"Then heard ring of bone..." -Lew Welch

McRedeye sez
Anarchy isn't a system
whole or incomplete
It's the absence of system
A vacuum that gets filled
immediately
Whatever's lying around
unattached
gets sucked in
Shiny new switches
cerebral chrome
& the whole thing
humming & throbbing
"in industrial ecstasy Let's come clean
Facts is facts Regardless of the subtle lint"
of one's collected beliefs
isn't one thing perfectly clear
The Army Corps of Engineers
gets things done

DE NATURA

More coyote than cuddly
Nature's wasteful & slow
Takes æons of time

& millions of failures
to get one thing right
"Humans are much more

efficient"
McRedeye sez
"And it's killing us"

CONTRA BOOKCHIN

Ecofascism echoes illogical. Sticks & stones
McRedeye sez, may break one's bones
But a monkeywrench

makes dents in armor. The bundle
doesn't get carried by the mob
pillaging

unless the tribe's alarmed
We have dog soldiers
& circles of sisters

who can surround evil
& smother it
with their bodies

like those Copper River women
who seduced the sentries
while the People

burned the invaders' stockade
Spanish buccaneers who'd drifted
north for plunder

In earth household cultures
it's the People themselves who
counsel to action -- every throat a voice

The task set us
born to Industrial Growthers
is ¡Viva βιος!

Learning to respect all living things
Even as we accept death's
housekeeping

Once again let the grandmas
dream the sacred. Remaking the world
hoops into baskets of plenty

Let the grandpas
tell into myth
the great mysteries

How Old Man Coyote
stuck a skyscraper
up his butt

& found Jesus
Or Batman. Or maybe
Kim Kardashian's glam lashes

If Earth First!
calls for earth
uber alles

it's in reaction to
earthfuck & earthfist
Adam Smith & the

Marx Brothers
Capitalists & commies
Osama & the Taliban

What's the real difference anyway
between all the -ism's
& their schisms?

Except perhaps those
tracking the chasm between
bound ions & free radicals

You don't need Enrico Fermi
to grok Bell's theorem -- that
mystical koan of the Atomic Age

Just this: that we are all
phase entangling
one body embraced

TO HELL YOU RIDE

McRedeye sez,
welcome to the club
we don't belong to

living near pricey Telluride's urban
outpost turned investment
bubblelonia

Most of us entranced
by unparalleled mountains
& unpopulated rural properties

Long-time worker locals
can hardly pay to stay
in T-town overnight now

Let alone own
a luxury home, a rental condo
or afford the taxes

No
you can't buy beauty
Just access to it

DOWNHILL SLIDE

Corporate ski. Corporate sky
Corporate private eye

It was the disembodied '80s
& money was moving in

By the time
McRedeye hitched
a ride To-Hell-U-Ride
the upwardly mobile were
on a downhill slide

Laying out lines
for Christendom's
high peaks

Even the slickrock's
strung out on uranium
& crystal meth

Calling it Scrapple
Pig's foot. A sow's ear

This
Southern Rocky Mountain
sacrifice area
turned
funky black op murphy bed

Lala-land for urban has-beens
& maverick haven't-beens
let out to grass

Imported valley cows
milking the elks' meadows

New Yorker cartoons
in dazzling Dali frames

All spilling over in freebox
funkadelic
Woodsies on pine sap
Yuppies in Gucci
Peaceniks & stockbrokers

But back then
anything seemed better than
another big stick bully boy orgy
of extractive looting
the 19th Century called
"striking it rich"

You dig up old wealth
Defang it
Then haul it away
to distant markets
as booty. As bounty

Today we use a gondola
Bring 'em here for
a bluegrass time-share film fest
Hoping for best of show

And yet
better trophy homes
than skulls on the trombe wall

Though what remains
is after all, far more invidious
than even that rogue Bulkeley Wells
could have dreamed of

Lighting up the San Juans
with centerfold color real estate
ads like big cigars

WINTER OF OUR DISCONTENT

Expected snow
& its band of flakes
a no-show

No surprise
It's the dosey-doe
of cloudless skies

This drumbeat of tax cuts
border walls, coal scat
& plutonium futures

It's undanceable
Unsustainable
An off-key bully boast

Care frozen mid-step
Wisdom in flaming absence
Face it, you're furious

Just realize it's anger
that makes the floor shake
Calls us out to act on

our thwarted liberal values
Mad as shaggy manes busting up
through the White House lawn

Disgust pushing us
onto the Beltway dancefloor
for a little Aztec two-step

A tarantella of protests is
the outside motion that comes
from an inside movement

Outrage that will not stay put
Though, as one dead poet
put it, to give us hope:

In every good tango
there's a step backwards too
Nevertheless, McRedeye sez

no time for tip-toeing. This ain't
the ballet. Best be joining hands
Jumping into the mosh pit

HAPPY EVERYTHING!

Spin the bottle
Bogart that joint
Party time

*Or immigrant times
mama, so many
fleeing for their lives*

The big operators
profiting of course from
empire. Making millions

Ah, but the privileged
too, sparkle out. Embers
to ash at Burning Man

Maybe hated
Maybe sated
satin & steel

Those of us rooted
Complicit by association
Maybe thriving

Own our own shelter
An insurance policy
Nursing a modest 401-K

Landed
along a rural off-blue
Colorado byway

The San Miguel Cañon
deepening into the
Dolores

             where we live with
         suffering & have learned, too
              to make our way

           up into Unaweep Cañon
              where the yellow
                monkeyflower

          unleashes its bee-syrup
            along the margins
                of the seep

              And yeah where
                  maybe
           a highway runs through

              McRedeye sez

   I dreamt I saw a bear ambling in the acorns
    across the grasses outside the meeting house
    entrée where I was admitting some young kids
    to a gathering that I was attending. I remember
   telling them on impulse, "Gotta watch out for bear"
   And looking across the conjured air, I saw not far off
    this big black boar nosing a grove of oak & piñon
     So, I pulled the two boys in & closed the door

ars POETICA

"Word spoken and note sung both enter the mind through that whorled and delicate fleshy gateway the ear. Poem written or song written come through the crystalline receiver of quanta the eye, in search of the inner, the mental ear … [T]he written word found a detour past both outer ear and inner ear to nonsensory understanding. A kind of short circuit, a way around the body."

–Ursula K. Le Guin, *Dancing on the Edge of the World*
(Grove Press, 1989)

FOUNTAIN PEN

Dip & scribble
Dip again
Pause. Reflect

& dip within
Skip dribble
& then dunk

Make pilgrimage
on random
paths

Stumble, roll
& right yourself
Self-amused

craft comes through
when fused
to wonderings

Imagine a
tea ceremony
played solitaire

McRedeye sez
In the random
calligraphy

of surprise
There's no
mistake

ON ONE'S OWN

A sudden fall's first snow
But it's expected

In politics
outcomes surprise ceaselessly
because one's ayes may be
the People's nay

No sure saddle
trotting the public nag

Poetry's simpler, McRedeye sez
It's all your stable
Your ayes

Fast strides. Clear skies

Ignore the papers' laurels
the labels they assign
or worse, libels in the zines

With verse
it's all your caper

IKKYŪ IN BERG'S
CROW WITH NO MOUTH

So nicely done, McRedeye sez
Ideograms flowering loose-leaf

   into couplets. Adept at
mimicking Japanese's elliptical

     association by location
Letting readers irrigate to

   whatever flow they want
Rimrock deluge or

arroyo's bedrock crumble
Black crow Red monk

YIN YANG

As one poet offered

"Sing like gentle breezes
among the leaves"

Or, as McRedeye sez

like a wind on fire
headed for the trees

A DICTION AIRY

Constantly writing
McRedeye sez, raw as sugar
cane. Bloody beets

Always refining
Mining the natural
for literature's elixirs

Distilling down. Yes!
Thousands of. Yes! Blooms
for a whiff of Blue Lily

ars PHILOSOPHIAE

"…in this world
you have to decide what
you're willing to kill."

–Tony Hoagland, *Donkey Gospel*
(Graywolf Press, 1998)

BOXTOP WISDOM ASIDE

"When you know that all is light, then you are enlightened."
—Yogi tea bag

Don't get me wrong
Enlightenment's great
especially for psychonauts

ballooning off into the ether
But, personally gimme
entheogenic embodiment

That's the nirvana
McRedeye seeks
Let the chthonic Goddesses

of Turtle Island & the Faerielands
grounded in deep mycelial touch
love me! Lick me!

Though sometimes charmed
in truth we're often played
by the great airy Olympians

To find a Pele
or a Kali Spiderwoman ally
root in the mud

The Great Gourd rattles
not with jizz
but with jazz

Who would prefer a mere wiggly
slice of light to the dancing
kernel's efflorescence?

And who would there be
to teach the tassels to sing
if not the mother stem?

HONEY
I GOT THAT ICE AGE HUNGER

Extinction's when they take
away your habitat, Rambo

Exterminators a la Schwarzenegger
take the shape of ruthless men

Rote machines. Natural forces
Earthquake. Tsunami. Erupting

volcanoes. McRedeye sez
eat while you can & re-use

aluminum. Recycle concrete
Re-invent Quetzalcoatl. But

let's face the music, As zig-zag
pell-mell chasing tail, shod hoof

& humping bull, we skidoo the Bear
Creek chutes of social self-destruct into

a dehorned glacial post-modern present
where -- whiteout! -- about all that

can be done gets done
in leafy rearguard stands

by warrior contraries like the Penan
Or in the dance of a few who store

& gather skills & songs
tools & seeds

For every split cord the cast-iron eats
smokes us a notch closer to midnight &

counting. Keeping time to angry Mother
Pele drummed up out of the Paleolithic

THE EDGE

McRedeye sez
even old coots love
the chase

Playing morning highway
rat race
with obstacles

in las curvas de los cañones

Rock
Deer
Semis

Fast pass. Broken line

Only braking
on blind curves

Riding the rail of
high speed
Hell
with the unexpected

Still
it's the
mountains

They know the rules

There's
no
stumbling

BEING

Reputation casts
shadows
dogs the heart

Sometimes laurel leaf
& sometimes
merde

While fame
tags along
turns heads

Is a kind of touch
Goldfingers!
And suddenly you're it

McRedeye
prefers
blue highways

Says
the less humans seen
the more human a being

DROUGHT

*"Nature's rasp never stops
rounding the edges"*
—Wu Xing

Just a frayed wick of
Moon leading Venus on
into a La Sal dusk

smudged over Paradox
with smoky hot clouds
teasing an absent monsoon

On my dry dirt
Cloud Acre walkabout
carrying hauled water

as plants & soil gulp
their once-a-day from
Wrenheim's Naturita overflow

McRedeye asks

Is an unexamined
life what is meant by
being here now?

PAGANUS

McRedeye claims he was trained
in the pre-Vatican II
Popish rites

Grew outraged by its excesses

Conversions
morphing into inquisitions

Oscar Romero assassinated

Sister Dianna Ortiz kidnapped
raped & tortured with cigarillos

He found his religion on a mountain

Tracking the dolorous wisdom of a crone
who sang the world back to Animism
& called it Deep Ecology

She prayed to the raspberries
& then preyed on them

BLOOD MOON

Blood moon eclipsed a moment
& now mid-heavens
full again

A friend emails a snapshot
"[So&so] said it was
God sending a message"

Whose fatwa ox
are we sacrificing here?
Good gods or bad gods?

McRedeye sez, So
anthropomorphic! Come on
gods are just gases on steroids

MORAL COMPASS AMBLE

Black cattle
in the fall grass east
White sheep west

Passing ducks thrash
across the pond
startled right

Through a canopy of piñon
a hawk flaps left
soundlessly

Walking
the county macadam
A no-snake-land

between Eve & Madonna
Loaf & risk
Decaf & malaria

McRedeye sez,
Dusk at the world's edge
Tomato bisque blood biscuits

OFFICIATING

Officiating
at a Telluride wedding
on Firecracker Hill

McRedeye lends an arm
to the bride on the way
upslope
only to be cast out
of Bear Creek's cathedral vestibule
after ceremony & signings

Immigrant life-rafts of leaves
aspen castaways
underfoot
like rice

Like old applause

As on the way up
so coming down

Alone
with what's been done

WHO WHO WHO

Sends chills up the spine
in line with the off-rhymes of
occasional minor thirds

Life's a lyric symphony
even as we move into
moving off

Maybe a festival
Sometimes just a gypsy fiddle
But always in tune

whether off-key or on
Delighted or defeated
we're privileged with choice

Grief's dark swoon
The ruff of laughter's feather swell
We can stop & join the chorus

Owls in the night canopy
Mystery sticking out its thumb
Mischief & joy's djembes

What point cash & cool?
McRedeye sez
Go hippie. Play the fool

ars ALLEATIeSIMBIONTI

"[M]ere purposive rationality unaided by
such phenomena as art, religion, dream
and the like is necessarily pathogenic
and destructive of life."

–Gregory Bateson, *Steps to an Ecology of Mind*
(Univ. of Chicago, 1972)

KINDOM CANTICLE

I started this George Oppen-influenced poem in the Cloud Acre john. It's a response to the first stanza of a wonderful lyric paean to the Pacific Rim by William Everson (aka Brother Antoninus). His "Canticle to the Waterbirds" begins with the marvelously cacophonous onomatopoeia: "Clack your beaks you cormorants and kittiwakes." His language is striking, alliterative, rooted in the earth. I made a Pagan Canticle which evolved into a scene in Craig Child's tenth annual Dark Night show in Paonia (CO) at the Paradise Theatre, "Emergent Kingdoms"

Unclap your millennial gates
& unhinge the heavenly armor
ye knights & bishops

The checkmate age of the sky
gods gone. No more lords
Melt the old swords

Enough of kings & courts &
benedicites before the killing sieges
Forget our specie's royal fist

The orchard opens up its stores
Each tree a throne
Each peach a prince

Each kami Kali spiderqueen
freely spinning silk
from out her own divine innards

Not caught in the web
but dancing the wind's harp

This rural canticle sung
yes, to raise praise on high
Holy! Holy! Holy!

But also to dig deep below
To be embedded
in the thick mud of the mystery

NO MORE
KINGDOMS!

Instead
let there be KINDOMS!

The fungal kindom. The floral
kindom. The faunal
kindom

where we hum the body's every bone
in honor of the making &
the yet unmade

All of us kin. Co-creators
In conversation, McRedeye sez
with what shines

And with those divine
goddess rhizomes
rooted in the deeper dark

where life springs
full-blown from
the spark of matter

TREE METAPHYSICS

Ponderosa pine
hold themselves
differently

Graceful. Rounded crown
& clumps of boughs
uplifted

Grounded. They take
their time
McRedeye sez

Linger on rocks
Sway in the breeze
& speak hot sparks

from their roots
deep in the sandstone
of the San Miguel Gorge

Spruce & fir
come to the point
quickly

Rarely burn
as other trees
do

North-facing.
Shallow-footed.
Alpine

Their needle limbs
focused on
a celestial apex

The wind sounds
heavenly
when they sing

TIPPING THE WORLD

As I remember it at last year's Shroomfest
there were big fields of pfifferling!
Whole slopes of chanterelles!

And maybe there were

"I remember" is a dangerous phrase
Science has walked us through this

What we observe. What we forget
What we add on to
each time we connect

But whatever was, or wasn't
McRedeye sez
this year let's re-make a memory
& start field cleaning on forays

Of course, going on a hunt
Finding for the feast

but post-picking & pre-eating
let's try sitting in-forest-situ

Ritually
brushing away debris
or wielding a knife to scrape off
detritus from cap & stem

There's more here than mere
hunter-gatherer etiquette
(important as that may be)

Field cleaning gives back
to soil's microbe-packed dispensary
a bit of what we've taken

Spreads the spores
Obeys the reciprocity of
original mind

And, truth be told, it's a coyote trick
to ensnare you into
that big picture moment

when, dropping
a bit off-balance into needles & duff
on fungi's front porch

you settle in
for strange mycelial memories
as their decomposing world
tips towards you

DEER

Deer, McRedeye sez
I sent you tumbling
into death in a barrow ditch

What karma goddess kami queen
comes now
panting at our heels?

CANNABALONEY

"Don't do Pot. Your brain will rot"
—anti-drug slogan

You hamburgers! McRedeye sez
Like my pack-a-day Dad
would always say

An oldschool Bay Area gardener
who ranted for years how cannabis
was the gateway to smack

But ended up before he died
growing primo bud
for his next door neighbors

A lesbian couple
who had him over for dinner
Invited him out for sushi

He tried their weed
But wasn't impressed
Nicotine his drug of choice

He didn't care about ganja
He cared for them
More than the risk of jail

The pot he grew
didn't rot their brains
It made them friends

NO DON'T DO THE NEW

It's what McRedeye loves
about cannabinoidal
enhancement

When properly used
you get to stroll
the casbah of the habitual

plucking mirrors off the shelves
Maryjane takes you away
Laos. Manaus

The Jud Wiebe Trail where
LaChapelle meets Neruda
& all get pleasantly lost

Or, if stressed, you find in yourself
the high-alert can-do
competitive edge

Doing it
Did it
Done!

Tho' best expect new operations
to come avalanche screeching
to a vertiginous halt

because your right
brain has gone galactic
faster than your left

brain can operate
heavy machinery
So, woo hoo

best chill & make peace
with the mutinously
altered

ENTHEOGENS TAKE YOU AWAY

What's to wait for?
McRedeye tells
the Red Monk

Sit
like you might never
get up again

Start that singing
inside
some call prayer

& others ayahuasca
Psilocybe
Cannabis sativa

Every chair
in death's waiting room
attaches to a sacred ground

Feel dirt's delirious electricity
feeding the quantum
flowering of

Higg's boletes
chanterelle quarks & whole fields
of hawkwing quasars

ars TOPOGRAFIE

"The first thing to do is to choose a sacred place to live in."

–Ernesto Cardenal, from "Tahirarassawichi in Washington"
Homage to the American Indian
(John Hopkins Univ. Press, 1973)

LOST COAST

Seen in McRedeye's wet dreams
a last lusty curve of horizon
untrammeled

Raw sand & surf's jaw-breakers
Dunes pierced with driftwood
like ocean earrings

Noxious gulls, wicked crabs
& the bare nervous necks
of beach deer

Bleached relic redwood &
washed-up Doug fir logs
big as legends

But no syringes
No oil spills. No
spewing sewer outlets

Just endless edge-
of-the-world
bluffs

waiting to be
rounded
& lured out to sea

Here on the Pacific Rim
that's anything but
peaceful, find restless

tides & rogue waves
Tokyo monster bubble buoys
Rope dragons & rusty bolts

Imagine hiking a still
mostly pre-industrial
orgy of wild

What
we used to call
California

CALIFORNIA

Crimson bougainvillea electric
against the painted cinderblock wall

One heavyset matron. Grandma
Ethnic mix. Alone in the park

Watches under an umbrella
her two charges. Boys. Little & small

Today's California is a pizza with everything
A landscape jumbled & out of place

as though Armand Vaillancourt was right
& his much reviled Embarcadero Fountain

at the foot of Market Street knelt
obediently at the cathedral altar

of the Golden State's future
dot.com culture chaos – all shook up

& tumbled on the earthquake
gameboard of the Pacific Rim

Exotic eucalyptus next to native redwood
next to peppertrees & valley oaks

lombardy poplars & date palms
Often in oddly planted rows in

shopping center parking lots. Suburban
yards. Alongside weeping willows

McRedeye sez
it's a place too beautiful to keep

Too crazy to last
Too dangerous to call home

COLORADO COYOTE

Just loping along
Nonchalant

As if traffic & trouble
didn't matter one whit

Broad daylight
by the Illium turnoff

Yesterday outside
the Telluride Museum

Same casual saunter
Brazen almost

Just as soon eat a housepet
as any wildass rabbit

Fancy fur coat
Sharp teeth

McRedeye sez
"My kind of dog"

SUNSET RIDGE

It was Ganci who said
"Life is a bowl of
cherry pits"

But he lived in a walk-up
in North Beach
Writing his way through hell

Attempting to rescue
God from the smothering
fleshy sweetness of Rome

I walk alone here on the rural
cusp of the Colorado Plateau
with its pitted roads

far from markets or
theaters or the human
conveniences of the century

High overcast clouds
break up on the Rockies'
muted gray like Whistler's

landscapes at the Cape
I can't see the moon
but in the half-dusk

she feels luminous
It's like I'm swimming in light
Immersed. Surrounded

Suddenly *La Luna* escapes
from the mist overhead
worshipped by stars

No need to kneel
McRedeye sez
Just see

WHITEOUT IN THE CANYON

Record snows
Gusting winds. Whiteouts
all evening

Had a raft of Oak Hill wrecks
on sheet ice. Luckily
no one hurt

Drove fearless
through the canyon
passing stragglers

until the blow turned
to blur & I too had to stop
Wait for a gust to pass

And then creep along
with both windows
open -- an eye

on the river's swerve
The other on the
cliff's rockfall ditch

Wipers going
slap slam lickety-split
A mechanical beatbox

I could feel flex
in every winter muscle
The mountains fierce

Inexorable. Cottonwoods
in sleet tights. Diaphanous
fairies turned furies

Nothing much to go on
McRedeye sez, 'cept
hunch & hope

MT. BLANCA

Sure, sugar
McRedeye sez
Let's climb it

Let's swing
peak to peak
over the wide San Luis

drenched in the hot
snowy blood of
Christ. Not

hung on a cross
but eating
combs of wild honey

in Mary
Magdalene's
bed

GUSTY WINDS

The gate bell gong
swings ding-dong to a
singalong sashay

Tremors shake elms
free of leaves. Cloud Acre's
shag & linoleum shiver

Window glass drums
& for strings
roof drain runoff

strums arpegglos
spilling over the lip of
a full barrel

I'm biting into a
Farmer's Market tomato
so knock-out sweet

McRedeye sez
its gusts trip me up
Tip me over

Add
my seedy breath to
autumn's first blow

SORCERER'S APPRENTICE

Even out here
in the frontier San Juans

Old Man Civ's power towers turn
desert curves into strutting grids

Marching buckets of coal
across the sagebrush swales

McRedeye sez, it gives
the upper Disappointment

on the backside of the Cone
a reason for its name

MEMENTO MORI

Cloud Acre
sinking
into the century

Spruce dying

Ponds going dry
in early spring

What's left us
of this time we have?

Gravity pulling the rug
out from under

Collapsing space
or inflating it?

As the solar wind
of our galaxy
Via Láctea

ups the ante
winding the primordial
into matter

"Whatever that means,"
McRedeye chimes in

"What matters is
a clock
that doesn't keep time"

13,019

I'm done with the Gregorian
McRedeye sez

Been on the scout for something
real to date my calendar from
Not imaginary births or pagan coverups

Since my family's made our home
on Colorado's Western Slope
let's begin our count
from the earliest artifacts found

What those Paleo folks
left us at Eagle Rock Shelter
along the banks of the Gunnison

Lithic relics
from 13,000 years ago
post-glaciation. Let's start there

But as Kuhn says of revolutions
best link the unknown
back to the known

So we can walk
that narrow bridge
into this new world

Add eleven millennia
to the current date &
leave the end years alone

SHIVAREE

Twenty years politicking
Running Green in a Red zone

Woke one morning to find
a dead coyote in the driveway

Front legs mangled where
the snowmobile ran it down

Dumped at Cloud Acre
on their way back from the forest

Elm poised in my front yard
watching me

watch the world
unload its venoms

I sing her a death song
rigid at my Lone Cone door

& wheelbarrow the bride
down to the willows

where the crows & the
skunks & the flies will feast

So much, McRedeye sez
depends on what we do

Shivaree: A rural Western American tradition involving a noisy mock serenade performed by a group of people to celebrate a marriage, often including ferrying the bride around town in a wheelbarrow.

Retired in 2016 after five terms as Colorado's only Green Party county commissioner, Art Goodtimes has won numerous awards for his political activism including from the Dept. of Interior, the Forest Service, conservative Club 20 of Grand Junction, as well as serving on dozens of boards and commissions on the local, regional, state and national levels. He co-founded the Sheep Mountain Alliance, Telluride's local environmental group, in 1988.

A former newspaper editor, he continues a weekly op-ed column "Up Bear Creek" in the on-line *MontroseMirror.com*, and a monthly op-ed column "Looking South from Lone Cone" in the Cortez-based *Four Corners Free Press*.

Art studied to be a Roman Catholic priest for seven years, and has continued to marry people as a Universal Life minister. He co-directs the Telluride Institute's Talking Gourds poetry project, is poetry editor for *Fungi magazine* (fungimag.com), and co-hosts the *Sage Green Journal* online literary anthology (sagegreenjournal.org). He was awarded a Colorado Council on the Arts poetry fellowship in 1989, has been poet-in-residence of the Telluride Mushroom Festival for 39 years, and was named Western Slope Poet Laureate from 2011-13. A long-time board trustee, he was founder of the Institute's Fen Advisory project and is director for their Ute Reconciliation program.

His latest poetry books are *As If the World Really Mattered* (La Alameda Press, Albuquerque, 2007) and *Looking South to Lone Cone* (Western Eye Press, Sedona, 2013). He was co-editor of the anthology *MycoEpithalamia: Mushroom Wedding Poems* (Fungi Press, CA, 2016).

A widower and a grandpa, Art lives at Cloud Acre on Wrights Mesa near Norwood with his two sons, Rio Coyotl and Gregorio Rainbow Oshá. His oldest daughter Iris Willow and his granddaughter Aurora Willow Fan live in San Francisco's Bernal Heights neighborhood, and his youngest daughter Sara Mac Friedberg makes her home in Telluride and works for the Telluride Science Research Center.

I want to be a gadfly on the ass of Socrates' nag